RAMEN
NOODLE
G E N I U S

Helpful hints

✳ To cook ramen noodles, boil them just until the strands separate *(about 3 minutes)* for tender noodles that aren't mushy.

✳ To coarsely crush noodles, leave them in their package and lightly break with your hands, or place them in a zippered plastic bag and use a rolling pin to finely crush them.

✳ To toast, heat oil or butter in a skillet and toss in broken noodles. Cook and stir until golden brown. Or drizzle with melted butter and bake at 400° for 10 minutes or until golden brown.

Copyright © 2015 CQ Products
Waverly, IA 50677

Printed in the United States of America
by G&R Publishing Co.

Distributed By:

Products

507 Industrial Street
Waverly, IA 50677

ISBN-13: 978-1-56383-526-1
Item #7113

Why Ramen Noodles?

* **Simplicity.** Open the package and they're ready to go.

* **Versatility.** These little guys can be used to make meals or snacks. Prepared with or without their seasoning packet, they can take the place of rice, nuts, other noodles, and sometimes even bread. But they easily stand on their own, too.

* **Convenience.** Grab some ramen from the shelf and start cooking. These handy noodles should become a permanent part of any pantry.

* **Speed.** When you toss ramen noodles into boiling water, you'll have perfectly cooked noodles in about 3 minutes.

* **Fun.** They're wiggly, they're jiggly, they're curly and fun!

* **Deliciousness.** They taste great!

Why not?!

Veggie-Noodle Stir-Fry

1 T. rice vinegar

1 T. sesame oil

2 T. soy sauce

2 tsp. hoisin sauce

1 tsp. brown sugar

2 tsp. minced garlic, divided

2 tsp. minced crystalized ginger, divided

2 (3 oz.) pkgs. ramen noodles, any flavor *(you won't use the seasoning packets)*

1 T. peanut oil

4 oz. fresh mushrooms, sliced

1 small head broccoli

½ red bell pepper, thinly sliced

Small handful of finely chopped fresh cilantro

2 green onions, sliced

DIRECTIONS

In a small bowl, whisk together the vinegar, sesame oil, soy sauce, hoisin sauce, brown sugar, and 1 teaspoon each garlic and ginger; set aside.

Cook the noodles in boiling water for 2 minutes; drain. Meanwhile, heat the peanut oil in a large skillet over medium-high heat. When hot, add the mushrooms, broccoli, bell pepper, and the remaining teaspoon of each garlic and ginger. Cook a couple of minutes until crisp-tender, stirring frequently. Stir in the cooked noodles.

Drizzle the set-aside sauce over the top of the noodle mixture and add the cilantro; mix it up well.

Top with the green onions before serving. **Serves 4.**

Chili Cheese Chicken

Preheat the oven to 400°. Set aside the seasoning packets from 1 (3 oz.) pkg. each chili-flavored and chicken-flavored ramen noodles. Cook the noodles in boiling water for 3 minutes; drain.

In a medium bowl, stir together the ramen seasoning packets, 2 C. shredded Monterey Jack cheese, 2 C. cubed cooked chicken, 1 (16 oz.) container sour cream, ½ C. sliced fresh mushrooms, 1 (4.25 oz.) can diced green chiles, 1 (2.25 oz.) can sliced black olives *(drained)*, and the cooked noodles.

Transfer to a greased 9 x 13" baking dish and sprinkle with 1 C. shredded cheddar cheese and ½ C. grated Parmesan cheese. Scatter 1 C. crushed chili cheese-flavored corn chips evenly over the top. Bake for 20 minutes or until browned and bubbly. **Serves 8.**

No-Bake Bundles

Cover a baking sheet with waxed paper; set aside. Melt 3 T. butter in a big skillet. Break 2 (3 oz.) pkgs. ramen noodles *(any flavor – you won't use the seasoning packets)* into small pieces and add to the skillet; toss to coat with butter. Cook over medium heat for 3 minutes or until noodles are golden brown, stirring constantly; transfer to a big bowl. Melt 1⅓ C. white baking chips and pour over the noodles. Stir in ⅓ C. coarsely chopped cashews and ⅓ C. dried sweetened cranberries.

With wet fingers, pack the mixture into a 2" cookie scoop and drop into mounds on the prepared baking sheet. Let set for 30 minutes. **Makes 18.**

Toasty ramen noodles are a great addition to these already-delicious flavors.

Potluck Broccoli Salad

2 (3 oz.) pkgs. ramen noodles, any flavor *(you won't use the seasoning packets)*

½ C. sliced almonds

⅔ C. canola oil

⅓ C. honey

⅓ C. rice wine vinegar

2 tsp. soy sauce

¼ tsp. sesame oil

Pinch of salt & black pepper

1 (12 oz.) bag broccoli slaw

1 (10 oz.) pkg. frozen edamame *(soybeans)*, cooked, cooled & shelled

½ C. thinly sliced green onions

1 (15 oz.) can mandarin oranges, drained

DIRECTIONS

Preheat the oven to 425°. Coarsely crumble the noodles and place on a rimmed baking sheet with the almonds, spreading them out in an even layer. Bake for 5 to 8 minutes or until golden brown, stirring occasionally. Remove and set aside while you make the dressing and salad.

In a small bowl, stir together the canola oil, honey, vinegar, soy sauce, sesame oil, salt, and pepper; set aside.

In a big bowl, combine broccoli slaw, edamame, and green onions. Fold in the mandarin oranges and noodle mixture; add the dressing and toss everything together until well mixed. Serve immediately. **Serves 8.**

Zesty Vegetable Soup

1 lime

1 T. olive oil

1 yellow onion, diced

2 carrots, diced

2 celery ribs, diced

1 zucchini, diced

Salt & black pepper to taste

1 (14.5 oz.) can diced tomatoes, drained

1 (32 oz.) carton vegetable broth

2 (3 oz.) pkgs. ramen noodles, any flavor, broken into quarters *(you won't use the seasoning packets)*

1 T. Sriracha sauce

¼ C. chopped fresh cilantro

4 green onions, chopped

DIRECTIONS

Zest and juice the lime; set aside while you make the soup.

In a big saucepan, heat the oil over medium heat. Add onion, carrots, and celery; cook 5 to 8 minutes or until soft. Add zucchini, salt, pepper, tomatoes, broth, and set-aside lime juice; bring to a boil. Stir in the noodles, reduce heat, and simmer for 3 minutes.

Remove from the heat and stir in Sriracha sauce and set-aside lime zest.

Top each serving with some of the cilantro and green onions. **Makes about 13 cups.**

Ramen, Sriracha sauce, and cilantro add a new twist to classic vegetable soup.

Twisted Skillet Pizza

Preheat oven to 450°. Set aside the seasoning packets from
4 (3 oz.) pkgs. pork-flavored ramen noodles. Cook the noodles
in boiling water for 3 minutes; drain.

Heat 2 T. olive oil in a big cast iron skillet over medium heat.
Add the noodles, pressing to cover the bottom of the skillet.
Cook until brown on the bottom. Remove from heat; spread
1 C. pizza sauce over noodles. Add layers of ½ C. shredded
cheddar cheese, 1 C. shredded mozzarella cheese, ½ (3.5 oz.)
pkg. pepperoni, 1 (4 oz.) pkg. Italian sausage crumbles, and
½ each red and green bell pepper *(diced)*. Sprinkle with
1 ramen seasoning packet, ½ tsp. Italian seasoning, and
½ C. shredded mozzarella cheese.

Move skillet to the oven and bake for 20 minutes or
until bubbly around the edges and the cheese melts. Cool
5 minutes before cutting. **Serves 4.**

Hot 'n' Spicy Snack Mix

Preheat oven to 400°. Break 2 (3 oz.) pkgs. ramen noodles *(any flavor – you won't use the seasoning packets)* into bite-size pieces and toss them into a medium bowl. Add 2 C. Corn Chex cereal and 3 T. vegetable oil; stir until well coated. Arrange in an even layer on a rimmed baking sheet.

In a small bowl, stir together ½ tsp. coarse salt and ⅛ tsp. ground cayenne pepper; sprinkle evenly over the noodle mixture. Bake for 10 minutes or until golden brown, stirring once halfway through baking time. Cool completely.

When cool, stir in 1 C. hot & spicy snack mix *(ours included nuts, sesame sticks, and crackers)* and 1 (12.6 oz.) pkg. peanut M&Ms. **Makes about 7 cups**

Swedish-Asian Meatballs

3 T. butter, divided

½ C. finely chopped onion

¼ C. milk

2 (3 oz.) pkgs. pork-flavored ramen noodles

1 egg

Salt & black pepper to taste

½ tsp. ground allspice

¾ lb. lean ground beef

¾ lb. ground pork

¼ C. flour

1 (14 oz.) can beef broth

½ C. sour cream

6 buns or hard rolls

DIRECTIONS

Preheat the broiler and grease a broiler pan. In a saucepan, melt 2 tablespoons butter over medium heat. Add the onion and cook a few minutes until softened. Reduce the heat to medium-low and add the milk; bring to a simmer. Finely crush the noodles and stir them into the milk. Remove the pan from the heat and set aside.

In a big bowl, whisk the egg, salt, pepper, allspice, and ramen seasoning packets until well mixed. Add the noodle mixture, stirring to combine. Crumble the beef and pork into the bowl and mix until well blended. Shape into 2" meatballs and arrange them on the prepared pan. Broil 4" from the heat for 5 minutes or until brown. Meanwhile, melt the remaining 1 tablespoon butter in the saucepan. Whisk in the flour until lightly browned. Gradually add the broth and cook until slightly thickened, whisking constantly. Stir in the sour cream and a little more salt and pepper. Add the browned meatballs and cook for 8 to 10 minutes or until they reach desired doneness.

Place meatballs and some of the sauce on buns. **Serves 6.**

Strawberry Spinach Salad

1 (3 oz.) pkg. ramen noodles, any flavor *(you won't use the seasoning packet)*

¼ C. sliced almonds

¼ C. sunflower nuts

¼ C. melted butter

6 T. sugar

¼ C. red wine vinegar

6 T. canola oil

¼ tsp. paprika

¼ tsp. salt

½ tsp. minced garlic

1 head Romaine lettuce

1 (5 oz.) bag baby spinach

1 pint fresh strawberries, hulled & thinly sliced

1 C. grated Parmesan cheese

DIRECTIONS

Preheat the oven to 400°. Slightly crush the noodles and toss them on a rimmed baking sheet with the almonds and sunflower nuts. Drizzle the butter over the top and stir it up until everything is well coated. Bake for 10 to 12 minutes or until nicely browned, stirring occasionally. Set aside to cool while you prepare the dressing.

In a small bowl, stir together the sugar and vinegar until dissolved. Add the oil, paprika, salt, and garlic. Mix well and refrigerate until ready to serve.

Tear the lettuce into bite-size pieces and put into a big bowl with the spinach, strawberries, and cheese. Toss to combine.

Divide into serving bowls and drizzle some dressing over each serving; sprinkle the cooled noodle mixture over the top. **Serves 6.**

Crunchy Noodle Bars

Preheat oven to 400°. Melt ½ C. butter in a 9 x 13" baking pan. Add 2 (3 oz.) pkgs. crushed ramen noodles *(any flavor – you won't use the seasoning packets)* and 3 T. brown sugar; stir to combine and spread in the prepared pan. Bake for 7 minutes or until bubbly and light brown.

Sprinkle with 2 C. mini marshmallows, 1 (11.5 oz.) pkg. milk chocolate chips, and 1 C. butterscotch chips. Bake for an additional 8 minutes or until marshmallows are puffy and golden brown.

Sprinkle with ⅔ C. each raw chip coconut and chopped walnuts. Bake 3 to 4 minutes more or until nicely toasted. Cool slightly and cut around edges with a sharp knife. Cool completely before cutting into bars. **Makes 24.**

Sweet & Sour Pork

Cook 2 (3 oz.) pkgs. ramen noodles *(any flavor – you won't use the seasoning packets)* in boiling water for 3 minutes; drain and set aside.

Heat 1 T. vegetable oil in a big skillet over medium heat. When hot, add ½ each red, green, and yellow bell peppers *(cut into chunks)* and ¾ C. diced cooked ham; cook until the peppers are crisp-tender.

Drain 1 (20 oz.) can pineapple chunks and reserve ½ cup of the juice; add the pineapple and the reserved juice to the pepper mixture along with ⅓ C. ketchup and 1 T. chili-garlic sauce. Toss in the noodles and stir to combine. **Serves 4.**

Ramen-Baked Spaghetti

4 (3 oz.) pkgs. beef- or pork-flavored ramen noodles

1 lb. Italian sausage or lean ground beef

1 onion, chopped

1 tsp. minced garlic

1 (32 oz.) jar spaghetti sauce, any variety

½ tsp. seasoned salt

1 tsp. Italian seasoning

2 eggs

⅓ C. grated Parmesan cheese

5 T. melted butter, slightly cooled

½ to ¾ (16 oz.) container ricotta or cottage cheese

3 C. shredded mozzarella cheese

DIRECTIONS

Preheat the oven to 350°. Grease a 9x13" baking dish. Cook the noodles in boiling water for 3 minutes; drain. Set aside the noodles and the seasoning packets while making the sauce.

Cook the sausage, onion, and garlic in a big skillet over medium heat until the meat is no longer pink, breaking it apart while it cooks; drain. Stir in the spaghetti sauce, seasoned salt, Italian seasoning, and two or three of the ramen seasoning packets.

Whisk the eggs in a big bowl. Stir in Parmesan cheese and butter; add the set-aside noodles, stirring to coat. Place half the mixture in the prepared baking dish. Top with half each of the ricotta cheese, meat sauce, and mozzarella cheese; repeat layers.

Cover with foil and bake for 30 minutes. Uncover and bake 10 minutes more or until the cheese is melted. **Serves 8.**

21

Chili-Lime Garlic Shrimp

6 to 10 frozen raw shrimp, thawed, peeled & deveined

1 T. chili-garlic sauce

2 T. soy sauce

½ C. sherry cooking wine

1 (3 oz.) pkg. shrimp-flavored ramen noodles

2 T. sesame oil

¼ C. sliced mini bell peppers

3 green onions, sliced

½ tsp. minced garlic

Juice of 1 lime

Chopped fresh cilantro to taste

Salt & black pepper to taste

DIRECTIONS

In a big bowl, stir together the shrimp, chili-garlic sauce, and soy sauce. Lay the shrimp in a single layer in the bottom of the bowl and pour in cooking wine to cover the shrimp. Cover the bowl and refrigerate up to 2 hours.

Drain the shrimp, reserving the marinade. Cook the noodles in boiling water for 3 minutes; drain. Set all aside.

Heat the oil in a big skillet over medium heat; add the bell peppers, onions, and the ramen seasoning packet. Cook for 30 seconds, stirring constantly. Stir in the garlic and cook for 15 seconds. Add the chilled shrimp and about half the reserved marinade; cook a few minutes until shrimp are pink and opaque, stirring often. Stir in the cooked noodles and the lime juice. Remove from the heat and stir in cilantro, salt, and pepper. **Serves 1.**

Cashew-Curry Chow-Chow

Preheat oven to 400°. Line a rimmed baking sheet with foil.
Break 2 (3 oz.) pkgs. oriental-flavored ramen noodles into a
big bowl. Add 2 C. cashews, 1 C. Corn Flakes cereal, and ½ C.
freeze-dried edamame *(soybeans)*; slowly stir in 3 T. vegetable
oil until well coated. Spread the mixture out evenly on the
prepared baking sheet.

In a small bowl, mix 3 to 4 tsp. curry powder, ½ tsp. ground
cayenne pepper, and the ramen seasoning packets; sprinkle
evenly over the noodle mixture and bake for 10 minutes. Let
cool completely. **Makes about 6 cups.**

*Seasonings really cling to clumps of ramen noodles,
and this mix is all about flavor and crunch!*

Twirly Latkes

Break 1 (3 oz.) pkg. chicken mushroom-flavored ramen noodles into three even pieces and cook in boiling water for 3 minutes; drain and dump into a medium bowl. Stir in ¼ C. grated onion, 1 T. flour, 1 beaten egg, ½ tsp. coarse black pepper, and the ramen seasoning packet.

Heat 2 T. each butter and olive oil in a big skillet over medium-high heat. When hot, drop a generous tablespoon of the mixture into the skillet for each latke, keeping a little space between each one; press down with the spoon to flatten. Fry on both sides until deep golden brown.

Drain briefly on paper towels. Serve hot with applesauce, sour cream, and/or green onion slices. **Makes 8 to 10.**

Little discs of crispy deliciousness.

Oriental Chicken Salad

4½ T. rice vinegar

4½ T. sugar

2 tsp. salt

1 tsp. black pepper

¾ C. plus 3 T. vegetable oil, divided

2 (3 oz.) pkgs. ramen noodles, any flavor *(you won't use the seasoning packets)*

1 (2 oz.) pkg. slivered almonds

1 chicken breast, grilled, shredded & cooled

1 head cabbage, chopped

¼ C. sunflower nuts

2 green onions, sliced

2 tomatoes, seeded & chopped

DIRECTIONS

In a small bowl, whisk together the vinegar, sugar, salt, pepper, and ¾ cup of the oil. Refrigerate until ready to use.

Heat the remaining 3 tablespoons oil in a medium skillet. Crush the noodles and add to the hot oil; cook until very light golden brown, stirring occasionally. Add the almonds and cook until golden brown, stirring constantly. Set aside until cool.

When ready to serve, combine the chicken, cabbage, and sunflower nuts in a big bowl. Stir in the cooled noodle mixture, tomatoes, and dressing, tossing to coat. Sprinkle the green onions over the top and serve immediately. **Makes about 12 cups.**

There's just something about toasted ramen noodles that makes a salad extra special.

Quick Shepherd's Pie

1 T. olive oil

1¾ lbs. lean ground beef

2 (3 oz.) pkgs. beef-flavored
ramen noodles

Onion salt, black pepper &
garlic powder to taste

1 carrot, cut into bite-size
pieces

1 onion, chopped

2 T. butter

2 T. flour

1 C. beef broth

2 tsp. Worcestershire sauce

½ C. frozen peas

1 tsp. paprika

DIRECTIONS

Heat the oil in a big cast iron skillet over medium-high heat.
Add the beef, the ramen seasoning packets, onion salt, pepper,
and garlic powder; cook until meat is no longer pink, breaking
it apart as it cooks. Drain and return meat to the skillet. Add
the carrot and onion and cook for 5 minutes, stirring often.

In a medium saucepan over medium heat, melt the butter;
add the flour and whisk for 2 minutes. Add broth and
Worcestershire sauce, whisking until thickened. Add this to
the beef mixture and stir in the peas.

Preheat the broiler. Meanwhile, cook the noodles in boiling
water for 2 minutes; drain well and arrange on top of the beef
mixture. Sprinkle with paprika and broil 6" from the heat
until the noodles are brown and crispy. **Serves 6.**

*No need to boil and mash potatoes for this
shepherd's pie.*

Grilled Bacon & Cheese

Cook 1 (3 oz.) pkg. ramen noodles *(any flavor – you won't use the seasoning packet)* in boiling water for 3 minutes; drain. Beat an egg; add the noodles and mix well. Pack the mixture into a greased sandwich-size container; chill 15 minutes.

Meanwhile, cook and drain 3 bacon strips; set out 2 slices each sharp cheddar and Muenster cheeses. In a small bowl, mix 2 tsp. mayonnaise, ½ tsp. Dijon mustard, ½ tsp. grated Parmesan cheese, and a pinch of coarse salt and pepper.

Melt a little butter in a medium skillet. Carefully tip the noodle square into the skillet and cook until brown on the bottom. Flip over and spread with the mayo mixture; add the cheese slices. Cook 8 minutes or until the cheese melts and the noodles are brown underneath. Remove from the pan, cut in half, add the bacon, and put the two halves together. **Serves 1.**

Cluck & Easy Dumplings

Slice 2 carrots and chop 2 celery ribs into a big saucepan. Add 1 (48 oz.) carton chicken broth, ½ tsp. ground white pepper, and 1 tsp. each chopped fresh thyme, parsley, and sage; cover and bring to a boil over medium-high heat. Reduce heat to medium-low and cook for 10 minutes. Stir in 1½ C. chopped rotisserie chicken and 3 (3 oz.) pkgs. roast chicken-flavored ramen noodles and their seasoning packets; cover and simmer while making dumplings.

In a medium bowl, mix 1½ C. biscuit baking mix with ½ C. milk and ½ tsp. each chopped fresh thyme, parsley, and sage until smooth; use a tablespoon to drop dough into 12 mounds on top of the noodle mixture. Cover and cook 10 to 12 minutes more or until a toothpick inserted into a dumpling comes out clean. **Serves 6.**

Ramen Chimichangas

1 C. diced onion

1 jalapeño pepper, seeded & finely chopped

Olive oil

2 tsp. minced garlic

2½ C. shredded cooked beef

1 (10 oz.) can chili-seasoned tomatoes

Salt & black pepper to taste

1 T. taco seasoning

1 tsp. ground cumin

½ tsp. lemon pepper seasoning

¼ tsp. ground cayenne pepper

2 (3 oz.) pkgs. beef-flavored ramen noodles

2 T. chopped fresh cilantro

3 C. shredded Colby Jack cheese

10 (8") flour tortillas

DIRECTIONS

In a big skillet over medium heat, cook the onion and jalapeño pepper in a little oil until they begin to brown. Stir in the garlic and cook for 1 minute. Then stir in the beef, tomatoes, salt, pepper, taco seasoning, cumin, lemon pepper, cayenne pepper, and the ramen seasoning packets. Reduce heat to low and simmer for 15 minutes, until most of the liquid evaporates. Meanwhile, cook the noodles in boiling water for 3 minutes; drain. Remove the beef mixture from the heat and stir in the cilantro.

Divide the cheese, the meat mixture, and the noodles among the tortillas; fold in two sides and roll up.

Place tortillas seam side down on a hot greased grill or grill pan and cook until golden on all sides. **Makes 10.**

Sirloin Stir-Fry

2 (3 oz.) pkgs. beef-flavored ramen noodles

1 lb. beef top sirloin steak, cut into thin strips

2 T. canola oil

2 T. soy sauce

2 C. beef broth, divided

2 (7 oz.) jars whole baby corn, rinsed & drained

2 C. fresh broccoli florets

1 C. diced red bell pepper

4 green onions, cut into 1" pieces

2 T. cornstarch

½ C. grated carrots

½ C. unsalted dry roasted peanuts

DIRECTIONS

Cook the noodles in boiling water for 3 minutes; drain. Set aside the noodles and the seasoning packets.

In a big skillet, cook the beef in oil over medium heat until no longer pink; drain off excess grease. Stir in soy sauce and cook 4 to 5 minutes more or until liquid has evaporated. Remove beef and keep warm.

Pour 1¾ cups of broth into the pan and sprinkle with the ramen seasoning packets; stir to blend. Add the corn, broccoli, bell pepper, and green onions; cook 5 minutes or until veggies are barely crisp-tender.

In a small bowl, whisk together the cornstarch and the remaining ¼ cup broth until smooth; add it to the skillet. Bring to a boil and cook 2 minutes or until thickened, stirring constantly. Remove the pan from the heat and stir in the beef, carrots, and set-aside noodles. Toss the peanuts on top just before serving. **Serves 4.**

Homey Chicken Casserole

Preheat oven to 350°. Slightly crush 1 (3 oz.) pkg. creamy chicken-flavored ramen noodles and cook in boiling water for 3 minutes; drain and transfer to a medium bowl. Add the ramen seasoning packet, 2 C. shredded cooked chicken, 1 (10.75 oz.) can cream of chicken soup, ½ (16 oz.) pkg. frozen mixed vegetables, and salt and black pepper to taste; blend well. Transfer to a greased 8x8" baking dish, sprinkle with 1 C. crushed Ritz crackers, and drizzle with 2 T. melted butter.

Bake for 30 minutes or until bubbly around the edges and the crackers have lightly browned. **Serves 4.**

Cinnamon Crunch

Preheat oven to 375°. Break 2 (3 oz.) pkgs. ramen noodles *(any flavor – you won't use the seasoning packets)* into small bite-size pieces and toss them into a big bowl. Add 5 C. Golden Grahams cereal, 3 C. Teddy Grahams, ¾ C. sliced almonds, and 1 C. golden raisins; set aside.

In a small saucepan over low heat, melt ⅓ C. butter. Stir in ⅓ C. honey and 1 tsp. orange juice. Drizzle evenly over the set-aside noodle mixture and toss to coat. Spread out evenly on one or two rimmed baking sheets. Bake for 10 minutes or until hot, stirring once or twice during baking. Spread out on waxed paper and let cool. **Makes about 12 cups.**

Several flavors come together in this recipe to make a sweet treat that's both crunchy and chewy.

Loaded Lettuce Wrap-Ups

2 (3 oz.) pkgs. Oriental-flavored ramen noodles

1 C. chopped rotisserie chicken

½ C. sliced green onions

1 (8 oz.) can sliced water chestnuts, drained

2 T. soy sauce

¼ tsp. ground cayenne pepper

2 tsp. sesame oil

¼ tsp. garlic powder

½" piece fresh gingerroot, peeled & grated

8 lettuce leaves *(like iceberg or Boston)*, washed & patted dry

½ cucumber, seeded & cut into thin strips

½ each yellow, orange & red bell pepper, cut into thin strips

Sweet & sour sauce

DIRECTIONS

Break both packages of ramen noodles in half and cook in boiling water for 3 minutes; drain, rinse with cold water, and put into a medium bowl. Mix in the ramen seasoning packets, chicken, green onions, and water chestnuts; set aside.

In a small bowl, stir together the soy sauce, cayenne pepper, oil, garlic powder, and gingerroot; add to the noodle mixture and stir to coat. Refrigerate until serving time.

At serving time, fill individual lettuce leaves with some of the noodle mixture; top with cucumber and bell peppers. Roll up tightly or serve "open-faced" with sweet and sour sauce. **Makes 8.**

Pork Tacos à la Ramen

4 (3 oz.) pkgs. pork-flavored ramen noodles

1 lb. ground pork

1 C. chopped onion

Vegetable oil

4 eggs

¼ C. flour

1 T. grated fresh gingerroot

1 T. minced garlic

Pinch of red pepper flakes

¼ C. soy sauce

1 T. sugar

2 T. water

2 T. rice vinegar, divided

1 T. sesame oil, divided

Juice of 1 lime

4 C. coleslaw mix

6 green onions, sliced

DIRECTIONS

Break each package of noodles into three pieces and cook in boiling water for 2 minutes; drain. In a big skillet, brown the pork and onion in a little vegetable oil over medium heat, breaking up the meat as it cooks. Set all aside.

In a medium bowl, whisk together the eggs, flour, and the ramen seasoning packets. Add the noodles and stir until well combined; let soak for 5 minutes. Remove the noodles from the liquid and set aside; pour the liquid into the skillet with the meat and cook over medium heat until egg is cooked, stirring constantly. Remove the meat mixture from the skillet.

Add enough vegetable oil to the skillet to cover the bottom and set over medium heat. When hot, scoop about ⅔ cup of noodles into the oil and spread into a 5" to 6" circle, making sure there are no holes. Fry for 2 minutes or until light brown on the bottom; flip and cook until brown underneath. Transfer to a paper towel-lined tray, fold the noodle circle in half, and stuff crumpled paper towels in the fold to hold the noodles in a taco shape. Repeat with remaining noodles; set aside to cool.

Discard most of the oil from the skillet. Add gingerroot, garlic, and pepper flakes; cook for 1 minute over medium heat. Stir in the soy sauce, sugar, water, 1 tablespoon vinegar, and 2 teaspoons sesame oil. When it begins to boil, add the meat mixture; stir to combine and remove from the heat.

In a medium bowl, stir together the lime juice, 2 tablespoons vegetable oil, remaining 1 tablespoon vinegar, and remaining 1 teaspoon sesame oil; add coleslaw mix and toss to combine.

Divide the meat mixture, coleslaw, and green onions among the taco shells. **Makes 6 to 8.**

Yummy Snickers Bars

3 (3 oz.) pkgs. ramen noodles, any flavor *(you won't use the seasoning packets)*

¼ C. butter

1 (16 oz.) pkg. mini marshmallows

4 fun-size Snickers candy bars, chopped

1 C. milk chocolate chips

1 C. peanut butter chips

¼ tsp. coarse salt

Crushed peanuts

DIRECTIONS

Grease an 8 x 8" pan. Coarsely crush the noodles and set aside.

Melt the butter in a big saucepan over medium heat. Add the marshmallows and cook until melted, stirring occasionally. Remove the saucepan from the heat; stir in the set-aside noodles and candy bar pieces until well coated. Spread the mixture evenly in the prepared pan.

Melt the chocolate chips and peanut butter chips together and spread evenly over the ramen mixture; sprinkle with salt and peanuts. Cut into bars when cool. **Serves 16.**

Why ramen? Why not? They're crunchy and they play well with other flavors like chocolate and peanut butter. The marshmallows are gooey, and that just adds up to awesome!

Pepper Jack Mac

Cook 3 (3 oz.) pkgs. ramen noodles *(any flavor – you won't use the seasoning packets)* in boiling water for 1 minute; drain. Rinse the noodles with warm water, drizzle with 1 T. olive oil, and toss to coat; set aside. Preheat the broiler.

Melt 1 T. butter in a big cast iron skillet over medium heat. Add 1 T. flour and cook until well blended, whisking constantly. Slowly add 1¾ C. milk; cook until slightly thickened, whisking often. Reduce heat to low; gradually stir in 2 C. shredded Pepper Jack cheese until melted. Stir in 2 tsp. Sriracha sauce, ½ tsp. salt, and ¼ tsp. black pepper. Turn off heat and stir in set-aside noodles. Stir in extra milk for a thinner sauce.

Place the pan under the broiler for a few minutes until it gets nice and brown. **Serves 4.**

Mini Vegetable Frittatas

Preheat oven to 350°. In a big skillet, heat 2 T. vegetable oil. When hot, add ½ red bell pepper *(chopped)*, ½ C. chopped green onion, and 1 grated carrot; cook a few minutes until crisp-tender and set aside.

Break 2 (3 oz.) pkgs. vegetable-flavored ramen noodles into four pieces each and cook in boiling water for 3 minutes; drain. In a big bowl, whisk together 6 eggs and the ramen seasoning packets. Add the noodles and the set-aside vegetables; stir to combine.

Using a ladle, divide the mixture among 12 greased muffin cups. Sprinkle each with shredded Parmesan cheese, if you'd like. Bake for 20 minutes or until set. **Makes 12.**

Chicken - Bean Burritos

1 (3 oz.) pkg. picante chicken-flavored ramen noodles

¼ C. water

2 T. lime juice

¼ tsp. black pepper

2 C. shredded cooked chicken

¼ C. thinly sliced green onions

4 (8") flour tortillas

Lettuce

1 C. corn salsa

½ C. shredded Mexican cheese blend

DIRECTIONS

Cook the noodles in boiling water for 3 minutes; drain and divide into four equal portions. Set aside.

Put water, lime juice, pepper, and the ramen seasoning packet in a medium saucepan and bring to a boil. Stir in the chicken and green onions.

Heat the tortillas according to package directions. Layer each tortilla with lettuce, one portion of noodles, ¼ cup of the salsa, ½ cup of the chicken mixture, and 2 tablespoons of cheese. Roll up and secure with toothpicks. **Makes 4.**

Ranch Ramen Chicken

3 C. water

½ C. chopped fresh broccoli

3 (3 oz.) pkgs. chicken mushroom-flavored ramen noodles, divided

1 T. cream cheese, softened

1 C. shredded cheddar cheese

¾ C. ranch salad dressing, plus more for serving

6 boneless chicken breast halves

Salt & black pepper to taste

DIRECTIONS

Preheat the oven to 350°. Coat a rimmed baking sheet with cooking spray; set aside. In a medium saucepan, bring water to a boil; add broccoli and boil for 1 minute. Coarsely chop 1 package of noodles and add to the saucepan with the broccoli; cook for 2 minutes, drain, and put into a medium bowl. Stir in the cream cheese, cheddar cheese, and one ramen seasoning packet; set aside.

Finely crush the remaining two packages of noodles in a zippered plastic bag, add the remaining two ramen seasoning packets, and shake to combine; transfer to a large plate. Pour ¾ cup dressing into a shallow bowl.

Pound each chicken piece to ¼" thickness; sprinkle with salt and pepper. Top each with some of the broccoli mixture and roll up tightly to hold filling. Coat with the dressing and then dredge in the crushed noodles. Arrange on prepared baking sheet, seam side down. Bake about 1 hour *(depending on size)* or until cooked through. **Makes 6.**

Chipotle-Lime Alfredo

¼ C. butter

½ C. heavy cream

1 (16 oz.) container plain Greek yogurt

2 T. sour cream

2 (3 oz.) pkgs. vegetable- or shrimp-flavored ramen noodles

¼ C. grated Parmesan cheese

2 tsp. southwestern chipotle seasoning blend (such as Mrs. Dash)

½ to 1 lime, zested & juiced

Olive oil

2 T. chopped fresh cilantro

2 T. shredded Romano cheese

DIRECTIONS

Melt the butter in a medium saucepan over medium heat. Whisk in the cream, yogurt, sour cream, and the ramen seasoning packets. Add the Parmesan cheese, seasoning blend, lime zest, and lime juice; cook for 1 to 2 minutes, whisking constantly. Reduce the heat to low and simmer 4 to 5 minutes, stirring occasionally.

Meanwhile, cook the noodles in boiling water for 3 minutes; drain and toss with a little oil. Add to the sauce and stir to coat.

Serve immediately with cilantro and Romano cheese. **Serves 2.**

Ramen noodles are perfect with this tangy Alfredo sauce.

51

Chili & Cheese Munch

Preheat oven to 250°. Break 2 (3 oz.) pkgs. chili-flavored ramen noodles into bite-size pieces and toss into a big bowl with 2 C. Crispix cereal, 1 C. cheddar cheese-flavored pretzel Combos snacks, 1 C. whole pecans, and 2 C. cheddar cheese-flavored Goldfish crackers.

In a small bowl, mix the ramen seasoning packets, ¼ C. vegetable oil, and 1 T. Worcestershire sauce until well blended; slowly pour over the noodle mixture, stirring until coated. Spread the mixture out evenly on a large rimmed baking sheet and bake for 1 hour, stirring every 15 minutes; cool. **Makes about 8 cups.**

Ramen Crunch Cookies

Preheat oven to 350°. Grease a couple of cookie sheets. In a big bowl, beat together ¾ C. softened butter, 1 C. sugar, 1 C. brown sugar, 2 eggs, and 1 tsp. vanilla until creamy. Blend in 2⅓ C. flour, ½ tsp. salt, 1 tsp. baking soda, and ½ tsp. baking powder until well mixed. Stir in 1⅓ C. Spanish peanuts, 1 C. semi-sweet chocolate chips, 1 C. butterscotch chips, and 1 (3 oz.) pkg. coarsely crushed ramen noodles *(any flavor – you won't use the seasoning packet)*.

Drop heaping teaspoons of dough onto the prepared cookie sheets and bake one sheet at a time for 12 to 15 minutes or until nicely browned. Let cool 2 minutes and then remove the cookies from the pan. Let one cookie sheet cool while the other is in the oven before adding more dough. **Makes about 6 dozen.**

Ramen noodle cookies? You bet!

Stuffed Bells

- 4 red bell peppers, halved & seeded
- Salt
- 3 (3 oz.) pkgs. pork-flavored ramen noodles
- 4 bacon strips, diced
- 1 onion, diced
- 1 (10 oz.) pkg. frozen chopped spinach, partially thawed
- ¼ C. water
- 1 C. shredded smoked Gouda cheese
- ½ tsp. coarse black pepper
- ¼ C. panko bread crumbs

DIRECTIONS

Preheat the oven to 350°. Arrange pepper halves cut side up in a 9 x 13" glass baking dish. Sprinkle a little salt evenly over the peppers. Cover with microwave-safe plastic wrap and microwave on high for 5 minutes or until crisp-tender; drain. Meanwhile, put the noodles in a zippered plastic bag and crush until the pieces are about the size of rice; set aside.

Fry the bacon in a big skillet over medium heat until done; drain off most of the excess grease. Add the onion and ½ teaspoon salt; cook until soft. Stir in the spinach, noodles, ramen seasoning packets, and water; cover and cook for 5 minutes or until spinach is thawed and excess liquid has evaporated. Transfer to a big bowl and stir in the cheese, pepper, and ¼ teaspoon salt.

Divide the noodle mixture evenly among the pepper halves, packing lightly. Sprinkle each with ½ tablespoon bread crumbs. Bake uncovered for 25 minutes or until peppers are soft and bread crumbs are toasted. **Makes 8.**

Broccoli Cheese Soup

1 T. vegetable oil

8 C. fresh broccoli florets

1 T. butter

½ C. chopped onion

3 C. chicken broth

½ tsp. garlic salt

¼ tsp. black pepper

2 (3 oz.) pkgs. chicken-flavored ramen noodles, broken into small pieces

3 C. milk

¾ lb. Velveeta cheese, cubed

DIRECTIONS

Heat the oil in a big saucepan over medium-high heat. Add the broccoli; toss to coat and cook until crisp-tender, stirring frequently. Remove the broccoli and set aside.

In the same saucepan, melt the butter. Add the onion and cook until translucent. Stir in the broth, garlic salt, and pepper; bring to a boil. Break the noodles into a few pieces and add to the saucepan along with the ramen seasoning packets. Reduce the heat to medium-low; add the milk and cheese, stirring until melted. Stir in the set-aside broccoli. **Makes about 15 cups.**

Broken ramen noodles are easy to eat with a spoon. Scoop 'em up and dig in!

Southwest Noodle Bowl

1 tsp. ground cumin

½ tsp. hot chili powder

½ tsp. lemon pepper
seasoning

Olive oil

½ lemon, juiced

Pinch of coarse salt

2 (3 oz.) pkgs. shrimp-
flavored ramen noodles

1 lb. frozen raw shrimp,
thawed, peeled, deveined
& patted dry

¾ C. guacamole, divided

1 T. chopped fresh cilantro,
divided

1 T. chopped fresh dill,
divided

1 C. halved cherry tomatoes

1 C. coarsely chopped
seeded cucumber

3 bacon strips, cooked,
drained & crumbled

DIRECTIONS

In a big bowl, mix cumin, chili powder, lemon pepper,
1 teaspoon oil, lemon juice, salt, and ramen seasoning packets.
Add the shrimp and toss to coat.

In a big skillet, heat 1 tablespoon oil over medium heat. Add the
shrimp and cook until pink and opaque. Remove from the heat
and set aside.

Cook the noodles in boiling water for 3 minutes; drain, drizzle
with oil, and put into a clean bowl. Stir in ½ cup guacamole,
half the cilantro, and half the dill.

Divide the noodles between two serving bowls. Top each with
half the shrimp, tomatoes, cucumber, and remaining ¼ cup
guacamole; sprinkle with bacon and the remaining cilantro and
dill. **Serves 2.**

Spam-a-Ram-a

Cook 2 (3 oz.) pkgs. oriental-flavored ramen noodles in boiling water for 3 minutes; drain and rinse with warm water. Drizzle noodles with 1 T. olive oil and toss to coat; set aside.

In a big skillet, heat 2 tsp. canola oil over medium-high heat. Add 1 (12 oz.) can of Spam *(cut into 1" chunks)* and fry until brown. Stir in 2 C. partially thawed frozen mixed vegetables and 2 T. soy sauce. Add 1 tsp. canola oil, the noodles, the ramen seasoning packets, and 1 tsp. black pepper; stir to combine. Make a well in the center and add 3 beaten eggs, breaking them up as they cook. Stir everything together until hot and well combined. **Serves 4.**

Why ramen? Why Spam? They simply make a great pair in this delicious meal.

Pineapple Flip

Preheat oven to 350°. Coarsely crush 1 (3 oz.) pkg. ramen noodles *(any flavor – you won't use the seasoning packet)*; set aside.

Mix 1 (18.25 oz.) pkg. yellow cake mix with other ingredients listed on pkg. to make batter, using the juice from 1 (20 oz.) can of pineapple rings plus enough water to equal the amount of liquid required. Pour 5 T. melted butter into a 9x13" baking pan; spread it around, coating the bottom and sides of the pan. Sprinkle 1 C. brown sugar in the pan and arrange the pineapple rings evenly over the top; add maraschino cherries as desired. Coarsely crush 1 (3 oz.) pkg. ramen noodles *(any flavor – you won't use the seasoning packet)* and scatter around the pineapple; pour the batter evenly over the top.

Bake for 40 minutes or until cake tests done. Carefully flip cake over onto a large serving plate, leaving the pan in place a few minutes before removing. **Serves 12.**

The Neglected *Seasoning Packets*

Four easy ways to use them deliciously.

Croutons

Preheat oven to 400°. Cut a small baguette into ½" cubes and toss with ¼ C. melted butter, 1 ramen seasoning packet *(we used picante chicken-flavor)*, ¼ tsp. dried basil, and ¼ tsp. ground cayenne pepper. Arrange on a rimmed baking sheet and bake for 15 minutes or until crisp and golden brown. Cool completely before using.

French Fries

Open a 26 oz. pkg. of frozen french fries and arrange on a rimmed baking sheet. Coat with cooking spray and sprinkle with a couple ramen seasoning packets *(we used beef-flavor)*, a little black pepper, and a hefty dose of chili powder. Bake according to package directions. Serve with cheese sauce.

Mushrooms

Toss a 16 oz. pkg. of fresh mushrooms into a slow cooker. Cut up ½ C. butter and toss into the cooker. Sprinkle with 2 ramen seasoning packets *(we used oriental-flavor)* and 1 tsp. dill weed; stir in 1½ tsp. soy sauce. Cook on low for 2 hours, stirring occasionally.

Garlic Bread

Preheat oven to 375°. Stir together 6 T. softened butter, 1 T. minced garlic, ½ tsp. dried oregano, ½ tsp. dried parsley, and 1 ramen seasoning packet *(we used chicken-flavor)*. Cut a loaf of French bread in half lengthwise and spread butter mixture over the cut sides. Bake for 12 to 14 minutes or until golden brown and crisp.